MW01200471

GIVE UP NEVER

FINDING TRUE VICTORY THROUGH PRAYER. NO MORE PULLING PUNCHES.

STEPHEN WOLLWERTH

Give Up Never

To all my kids: My prayer is that you live a completely different life than everyone else. Don't be normal. Pursue God with tenacity... too few people do that. Do what's right. Learn to take everything to God in prayer. Realize that I never really lived until I started pursuing God daily; that's when I came to life. I want to change the world, but I know that you can do even more. When you face the difficulties in this life, tackle them with prayer.   When you have a dream to accomplish something, make sure it's huge, and pray it through.

To my precious wife: Thank you for always believing in me. You really are perfect. Thank you for having so much faith in God and believing with me for miracles. We ain't seen nothin' yet!

Contents

WHAT IS VICTORY?

The subtitle of this book reads, "No more pulling punches." It's a boxing term: when you pull a punch, you don't hit the other fighter as hard as you can. It also means to hold back from doing what you think you should do. (urbandictionary.com) Many missed victories are the result of pulling punches, whether in work, business or our spiritual lives. We don't meet the challenges with enough force to cause a reaction. We hold back, because we doubt, or we've seen too many failures around us to believe we can do more than just make it through. Why is the "NEVER" on the cover written in crayon? My 8 year old son Judah wrote it. It signifies a childlike faith that won't give up. I had a different title in mind for this book, but one day I asked my son Jacob what he thought the title should be. He said. "I know! I know! You should call the book 'Give Up' and have a child's handwriting write the word 'NEVER' in crayon across it." WOW. That's wisdom from a child who understands faith.

As I think about the
potential audience for
this book, I really want
everyone to read it,
regardless of whether or
not you believe in God. I
believe that the principles
found in this book have

> **"If you're going
> through the
> desert, don't build
> your house
> there."**

merit for any person desiring to overcome difficulties
they might be facing. It's out of a sense of compassion
and a desire for an overcoming spirit for all people that I
write this book. For those not used to reading a book
with Bible verses quoted in it, or mentioning spiritual life,
I would like to invite you to grab what you can from it to
help you overcome what you're facing. It's an invitation
into what has helped our family have total victory over
some of the darkest moments in our lives. Maybe you're
facing a bad diagnosis from the doctor, or maybe you're
struggling in your mind with anxiety – whatever the case,
you need to get through the circumstance saying you
had victory... and I want to help you get there.

To those who already profess faith in Jesus, I'll start
by saying that the lives of those who believe in Jesus
are supposed to be marked by many traits that those
who don't have faith in a supernatural God do not have.
One of those traits is being victorious in every situation.
Romans 8:37 states, "No, in all these things we are more
than conquerors through him who loved us." We are
more than conquerors- MORE than conquerors! But
often times there doesn't seem to be a difference
between the life and level of victory between one who

believes and one who doesn't. I believe the main reason for this is that many believers never grab hold of the truth that they can have as much of God's presence as they want. The fact is that most Christians just don't pursue closeness with God. Like Moses on the mountain, who was gone for weeks spending his every moment in God's presence, that his face shone with God's glory, we can also gain an evidence of God's glory when we pursue him.

I heard a profound statement once, "If you're going through the desert, don't build your house there." If you have found you have accepted the plight of your bad situation, and have laid down your will in place of the will of the negative circumstance, but you're looking for a way out, this book is for you. It's a guarantee that at some point in your life you're going to feel stuck in the desert. I felt stuck in the desert when my eight year old son had lupus. I felt stuck in the desert when my business failed at the exact same time our landlord was moving back into our rented house, putting us nearly on the streets. I felt stuck in the desert the day I was laid off from my job in 2008. The fact is, because we are more than conquerors we should fully expect to overcome these situations in due time, but overcoming requires the same mentality and actions as an overcomer and a conqueror. And overcoming is not the same as "just getting through". What do conquerors do? They fight. I've been in too many Bible studies and prayer meetings when prayer requests are mentioned for serious issues, and the response is hanging heads, groaning and sighing as if we've already been defeated and broken. No! It's time to stand on the word of God; we are not defeated! Miracles still happen, and I've seen them with my own eyes.

When you find yourself in the desert, and perhaps in despair, it's time to seek the Lord for what you can learn while you're there, and to fight like a conqueror and claw your way out of that desert. I believe every negative situation in life should have a testimony of victory at the end of it. Why do I think that? In my life I can tell you a miracle story at every crossroads, not just a story that says, "But we finally got out with our shirts still on our backs." Rather, our testimony says, "Look at the miracles that came about from it!" That son who was diagnosed with an autoimmune illness, he's completely healed. That time we lost our home, we obeyed God, moved across the country and have thrived ever since. That time in 2008, when I got laid off, I prayed like never before and within two days got hired for a new job with twice the pay. You'll read about all of these testimonies.

This is a book about victory, a really overcoming victory, and the mindset and actions needed to obtain victory. In these next chapters you'll see how God answered prayers in undeniable ways in our lives. And through reading these stories, your faith will begin to grow and you can become victorious too, through prayer. There's no more playing around. The enemy hates you and he isn't embarrassed to come against you, so let's not be embarrassed to pursue God like never before and obtain the victorious life He intended us to live. No more pulling punches.

CHAPTER 1

PRAYER...JUST START!

When I was 35 years old, I was full time Media Director and Music Director at a church in South Carolina. The pastor came to the staff and board one day and challenged us to do something unusual. He challenged us to spend the next 30 days praying and reading the Bible for 3 hours each day and see what would happen after that period of time (for those who could be so disciplined to complete the task). I grabbed the challenge wholeheartedly. For the next 30 days I got up early, perhaps 2 to 3 hours earlier than usual. I would put my headphones on and run while it was still dark, listening to the Bible from YouVersion®, then since I ran so far from home, I would walk the rest of the way home praying. Each day the process would take about 2 ½ hours. I would spend another half hour in prayer at a different time in the day that was convenient.

This challenge should have been titled '30 Days to Make You Realize You Haven't Lived, Yet'. I loved every minute of that challenge! I began to feel I was getting so close to God, and I began to hear his voice like I never had previously in my life. I had been a "Christian" since I was young, but during this prayer challenge, I honestly felt like I finally woke up from an entire life of slumber at age 35. I began to see answers to prayers instantaneously as if God was saying, "YES! This is how I want you to live! In my presence constantly!" The 30 days were so amazing, I never stopped. I've had periods of busyness which prevented 3 hours a day in prayer, but they didn't last forever. I've continued this pattern of long periods of time seeking God for the past 6 years. Just this morning, I spent about an hour and a half in prayer.

Prayer used to seem boring to me, but it became all I wanted to do. I'm a type A personality and love action and activity. So becoming a person who loved prayer seemed strange until I found out what prayer was really like. I discovered that it doesn't matter what prayer looks like. You can pray while running in the morning, walking to work, biking on a trail, sitting in your living room, standing in the shower, kneeling in a closet, hiding under a blanket, pacing the halls or shouting at the sky in the middle of a forest. So I encourage you to erase any notion that prayer can only be kneeling on a bench in a cathedral. My greatest suggestion is that prayer be purposeful, dedicated and time set apart. Through discipline and obedience, I began to see the results of fervent prayer. It was like going to the gym, and after a month, seeing huge physical results like defined muscles and a lean waist, except these results were tangible in many other ways.

God began to show me that His purpose is to use me to change the world, not just give me what I need.

Answers to prayer became so frequent and so quick, that I was surprised when I had to wait any amount of time for an answer to a problem. I'm going to warn you that these first few examples of answered prayer in no way mean that I support a prosperity doctrine in which all your prayers lead to money. It just so happened that God showed me his power through answered prayer in my finances first. I promise, we'll talk much more about things more important than money in just a bit. One of my first most notable answers to prayer was as follows.

I ran a video production company part-time in South Carolina at the time, and some of my income was dependent on contracts with companies. On one particular occasion, I remember realizing that if I didn't have a deposit that very day, we might be in a financial pickle by later the next week. So I prayed, "God, I see our bank account getting low, and I know that if I'm going to make it this month, I need to be able to send an invoice for a contract TODAY!" There were no projects really in the hopper that I could think of. So this prayer was pretty audacious. To be able to send an invoice without a current project was a stretch. I prayed with fervency and faith, knowing that God would provide. I prayed this prayer at around 7:30am that particular morning, then I went about my day. At 10:00am I received an email from a company that I had placed a bid for a particular video contract. I was waiting for their reply as it had already been several weeks since I sent the quote. The reply said that they were ready to start on the project. The contact at the company actually said "If you would like to send an invoice for the deposit, that would be fine." Boom! Answered prayer. On another occasion I was bemoaning the fact that our backyard had no grass, just dirt. I had been trying for months to get grass to grow. I had been planting, seeding and fertilizing, but the conditions weren't right for some reason and nothing would grow. So I prayed while I was jogging one day during my prayer time, "God, I can't make grass grow in that dry dirt, and I can't afford the sod, but I know you can. Please, just make grass grow in the backyard." Two days later, I got a phone call from my friend Chris that the local high school was digging up their football field and giving all the sod away. My friend loaded a bunch on his truck and brought it to my house. Boom! Instant lawn, answered prayer! My kids and I played on that grass for years after that. There was even enough left over to bless my neighbor with grass around her group of trees next to my yard.

On another occasion, we were in need of some additional lighting for video production. Professional lighting for video production on the cheap end can be around $600 for one studio light... and we needed three or more lights. I said to my colleague, "Let's pray. God knows we need this equipment and He can provide it." So he and I prayed together in the office that day. We declared aloud that we knew God was able to provide and we asked that God would miraculously provide the lighting we needed. We never mentioned to anyone our prayer request. It was just between God, my colleague and me. About two days later, I received a phone call from a friend that was a director for a TV station. He said to me, "Steve, you need to get down here to the TV station. It's closing down and all this equipment is going to go to waste, never to be used again. Come on down and see what you guys can use." Wouldn't you know it, there was a bunch of lighting equipment available for us to take! So we loaded it up in the car. It was exactly what we needed.

These answered prayers were just the beginning of my understanding of gaining victory in just small circumstances. They would also train me to grow in my faith to help other people in the future in ever increasing scale. Through these experiences of answered prayer, God began to show me that His purpose is to use me to change the world, not just give me what I need. So God began to teach me to pray with the faith that realized that we were made to bring about God's will on earth, and begin to pray for greater things, earth-impacting types of prayers.

In early 2012, my wife and I visited the Philippines. Her hometown is Iligan City on the southern island of Mindanao. Just three months earlier, a tropical storm came through with such force that the floods from the rains killed more than 1,200 people and the swollen rivers swept away or damaged the homes of more than 700,000 people, (according to the National Disaster Risk Reduction and Management Council in the Philippines on February 2012). We arrived on a vacation, but soon the trip turned into a mission. We visited the ravaged areas and saw the difficulties, the homeless children, tents as far as the eye could see, where displaced families were living. We knew we had to do something. I had my camera with me, and I began to shoot a documentary so word could be spread about their difficulties. With faith that God could use the documentary, I began to work on it when we returned to the States and began to push the story on social media. We believed that God wanted to use us to help these displaced and homeless people, so we prayed like we believed that. A few months passed and we were able to raise $20,000. Property was donated by my wife's uncle who is a local pastor. And the Iligan government partnered with all of us on this, and added enough funds to build houses for 52 families.   Additionally, my wife began to plan a second trip with a medical team to come back in a few months to help with the people's needs.

About ten days before the trip, we had one major problem. We didn't have sufficient funds for the airfare, or for the medical supplies to take to the Philippines. What happened next forever changed my view of God and His interaction with those who pray. That day was no different than any other. I got up early to pray and seek God. One of my major prayer requests was for the funds necessary to make the trip and for the medicine and other supplies. My prayer time was over in a little more than an hour and I went on my way to work.   At about 2 pm that afternoon, feeling a bit discouraged that no progress had been made that day, I decided to have a second prayer time and really ask God for what we needed. After all, my wife was supposed to leave in 10 days to lead this trip and we had no ticket and no supplies.

I went out to a usual spot to pray under a large live oak tree in a field with no one around. As I began to pray, I began to shout to heaven. I said to God, "GOD, LOOK AT ME! Haven't I always been faithful with finances and giving to those in need!?" I started to run across the field waving my arms up in the air screaming, "God look at me! Look at me!" I pleaded with God in desperation to send us the funds miraculously. I said loudly, "I need $10,000 to take care of all these needs!" I prayed with a fervor and intensity that if anyone had seen me, they would have thought I was crazy. This type of prayer lasted about 10 more minutes. As I wrapped up my less-than-dignified prayer time, I began to walk back to my office. As I was walking, my phone rang. It was a good friend Scott, a very prayerful man who I've always known to live his life full of faith. His first words to me on the phone were in a confused tone, "Steve? What's going on?" I answered, "What do you mean what's going on?" Still in a confused tone, he said, "Steve, God just told me to write you a check. How much do you need, and what's going on?" Without any hesitation I replied, "Scott, I need $10,000." He was taken aback by such a huge number. "You need what!? Hold on a minute, I'll call you right back." About 10 minutes later, he called back. "Steve, I don't have $10,000," he said, "but I'm writing you a check for what I have. I'm sending you $4,586. I'm putting the check in the mail. You'll have it by the end of the week."

By the end of that week, I had also won a contract with an ambulance company for a project that would take two weeks and I would net an additional $11,000. It was the largest contract I had ever had for such a short time period. God heard the prayers of one man pouring his heart out in a field in one town, and at the very same moment, spoke to another man 50 miles away telling him to be the answer to that prayer. Simultaneously, God worked out the details of a large contract which ultimately paid more than enough for all the needs of the missions trip. From that moment on, I knew beyond a shadow of a doubt that God heard my prayers and was alive and actively involved in my life. I could always come to Him, and know that He "rewards those who seek him", Hebrews 11:6.

Imagine if I had never started on this prayer journey, we would have never had the faith or even the thought process to pray in a way that God could use us to touch a city in the Philippines. On that medical trip, my wife and those doctors, nurses and community organizers ministered to more than 1,000 patients, helping with physical needs and sharing the Good News of Jesus with them. All the houses are now built and families have moved in.

The journey of seeking God diligently started with that 30 days of dedicated prayer. I would have never seen God's purposes fulfilled to the depths that they have been if I hadn't started on that journey. We got beyond the typical prayers of the average American Christian. We were beyond prayers for bills to be paid and for house payments to come through. We began to pray for larger, kingdom-of-God issues, for God to use our lives to change people's futures, to bring broken families back together, to build homes for homeless people in other parts of the world, to bring orphans home to their forever families and to see sickness and disease run away.

You'll see in the coming chapters the progression of the barriers and difficulties that I prayed through. These first stories are just the beginning, and they're really just external physical provisions that God can so easily provide if we just ASK and BELIEVE. There are deeper victories that require a different level of perseverance and prayer that we'll dive into, but the key to it all is that YOU MUST START TO PRAY. It's like lifting weights. Every bodybuilder started small, and there was a day they decided to strengthen themselves, working diligently day by day. Let's make TODAY the day you start to pray. It will be the beginning of a life filled with victory!

CHAPTER 2

SOMETIMES YOU HAVE TO STEP OUT

Sometimes the answer to our overcoming and breaking through to a victory takes more than prayer. Sometimes we have to be willing to partner with our Father and step out in ways that look crazy. This is what happened in one of the most amazing answers to prayer that I've experienced in my life. But I have to give you a little background on this particular situation.

Over the course of my short life, I've given away a lot of stuff to people who needed it. I gave away my first car when I was 20 years old. I had received an inheritance from my dad who died when I was ten years old, and I had just received the money that year in college. My music professor David was driving to the university one cold Minnesota day, and his wheel fell off his old Honda Accord, leaving him stranded in a not-so-good part of town. This was just a few weeks after he had major engine trouble for the second time, with costly repairs. He had 3 kids at the time and I felt such compassion for his situation that I decided to give him $5000 of my inheritance. Needless to say, my mom was pretty upset about my decision. As a parent, I don't blame her now for being upset. When I gave the money to my professor, he said to me, "I don't want to take this money from you, but God won't let me refuse it." With the money, he was able to buy another used low mileage Honda Accord, which he used until I graduated.

Over the next 18 years, I gave away another 4 or 5 cars. On one occasion I gave away a minivan to a guy who needed transportation to start a new business. I also gave him a lawn mower, a weed wacker and a blower so he could get his landscaping business off the ground. This is all just background and a preface that God never forgets your generosity to others.

Giving away our minivan caused our family to be in need... and just like those families and individuals that needed a miracle, we needed a miracle as well. I was convinced that God didn't want me in debt, so although I could afford to make another car payment, I didn't want to do that. I began to pray once again, for God to do a miracle. Each day, I drove by the Honda Dealer in our only car and looked at the Honda Odyssey minivans. To me, the new Odyssey was just the most amazing vehicle ever for a family and a business (and the black one was even cool for a guy to have). One day as I was praying for a vehicle, I sensed that God asked me a very direct question, "What kind of car do you want?"

My response to this question was answered in my usual honest way. I answered, "Well, since you're asking...I would like a black Honda Odyssey, with leather, navigation and an entertainment system with a DVD player." Then I felt the Lord say to me, "Then ask Me for it." And so, emboldened by the fact that God asked me what I wanted, I began to pray for that.

For a period of about 3 weeks, I would go to the dealer after hours at night and pray over the Honda Odyssey with those features. I would circle it, declaring that it was mine in Jesus' Name. One night as I drove into the parking lot of the dealer, I was sad to discover that it had been sold. There were no other black Odyssey vans on the lot with leather. So I waited until they received a new shipment, and when it finally came on the lot, I started circling and declaring that THAT one was mine, and NOBODY else could have it. I brought the family out there, we all put our hands on the van and prayed that God would provide it for us.

The difficulty you're facing may require you to listen to that instruction from God telling you to do something a little outside the box.

On a Friday morning, as I was getting ready for the day, the most ridiculous thought crossed my mind, a thought so crazy I just knew it was God speaking to me. I heard the concept like a voice telling me the whole idea. "Go to the Honda dealer, find the general manager and say this, 'I would like to produce your commercials for your dealership, but I don't want you to pay me. Instead, I want to trade my services for a vehicle.'" You see, I had been producing videos for a few companies, nothing huge, so this opportunity would be a big step up for my business. So with a crazy faith that God had really instructed me to do this, I drove to the dealership, walked in and asked to speak with the general manager. As it turns out the general manager knew who I was, and invited me to sit down in his office. I sat there with this nervousness like when you're about to ask someone to marry you. I was trying to keep from shaking as I spoke. So I said to him the exact thing I was instructed to say. After showing him a little of my video production portfolio, I asked him if I could produce their commercials but instead of receiving payment with money, I wanted that black Odyssey sitting right outside. Mike, the general manager paused, looked up and said, "I think we can work something out. You see, we just had a meeting and were discussing who was going to be our spokesperson in the coming year as we build a new facility. It looks like this is perfect timing!" So that day, I walked out of the dealership with a contract to produce their commercials monthly, and a brand new black Honda Odyssey with leather, navigation and all the bells and whistles. It was the perfect vehicle to represent my business and carry my growing family.

I can't tell you the feeling that day when the impossible happened and I drove off the lot in that $42,000 van. What God was showing me during those formative times of prayer was to believe Him for impossible things. Don't limit God and what He is desiring to provide for those who are faithful to Him. In addition, I needed to see that sometimes the answer to a need would require obedience on my part in order to see the results. God won't make a car appear in my driveway but He will provide miraculous connections, if I'm willing to step out. Once again the Bible talks about co-laboring with God in 1 Corinthian 3:9. He gave us hands and feet and a brain so we could use them for His benefit, and also to provide for ourselves and families. So the difficulty you're facing may require you to listen to that instruction from God telling you to do something a little outside the box. But you won't hear that small voice until you begin to pray so much, that His voice speaking to you becomes a daily occurrence.

CHAPTER 3

AUTOIMMUNE ILLNESS

Three years ago, as we drove into California in our Ford RV, we had begun a new chapter in our lives. We were stepping out to see God's plan unfold in a new place. It took us ten days to drive across the country, firstly because I really don't like driving long distances. And secondly, my wife was 7 months pregnant. One night on that journey, as my son Jacob (who was seven at the time) was getting ready for bed I saw a little mark on his backside. It was pretty small and it looked like ringworm. We didn't get too concerned about it. We just thought we would grab some over-the-counter medication from the pharmacy at some point. (No big deal, right?) Within the next few weeks that mark on his rear grew larger and larger despite us putting medicine on it. Then one day I saw the same type of mark show up on his upper arm. A few days later the mark was also on his left arm, then his forearms, then his back. About three to four months after we arrived in California, Jacob's entire body had these little marks on it, and what's worse, they were growing much, much larger. We thought maybe he had an allergy to some new food in California, so we started experimenting with his diet. Gluten free was all the craze, so we tried that, too. Jacob had started his first year of public school, and because of the rashes, he had to wear a hat, long sleeves and long pants even in the hot California climate . Life was becoming more and more difficult for Jacob, but he was handling it amazingly. He hardly ever complained about anything, although we found out much later how much he struggled internally with the inconveniences.

One morning as Jacob was getting ready for school, I noticed a little dot on his face. The same little dot that each rash on his whole body started from. Some of the rashes had grown into rings that were 4 inches around on the other parts of his body, so it was likely that this dot would turn into a large ring, too. I had enough. I scheduled an appointment with a dermatologist. At the appointment, the dermatologist looked at his skin with a very confused look on her face. She said she had never seen anything like this in her 16 years of practice as a doctor. She gave us some stronger topical medication, and suggested a trip to a pediatric dermatologist. After a month of using this medication, he was no better, in fact, he was much worse. So we scheduled another appointment with a pediatric dermatologist. At that appointment, at the doctor's advice we decided to do a biopsy on the first lesion and have a bunch of blood tests done. Jacob was brave as could be having needles stuck in him and a biopsy done. We treated Jacob to whatever food he wanted after those painful tests, which cheered him up a bit.

> **The words we use over a circumstance are very important. What we say indicates what we believe and what we expect. What we focus on is always what we will achieve.**

We got the test results back and they weren't good. His blood had very high levels of antinuclear antibodies (ANA) and high SSA levels as well. Doctors explained that these results could be indicators of Sjogren's syndrome, Graves disease or systemic lupus. But they suggested we see a pediatric rheumatologist at UCSF. Each of the potential diagnoses pointed to an autoimmune illness. I know for some of you reading this, this language is all too familiar. A flood of darkness and a quickly growing confusion and despair began to overtake us. "Not my son!" was my heart's cry. "How could this be happening to us?" I remember the feeling that day. It was probably the most terrible darkness we've ever experienced.

But then I remembered something. I'm a person of faith in God, we have seen other miracles, other answered prayers. I've built my life on trusting God and the truth of His word. We've experienced other victories in our lives on smaller scales, and now we would have to press in praying again to see a victory in this as well. All that I've learned from my times of prayer and trusting God for miracles was being put to the test now. Do I believe Him, or do I fear? Thankfully the scripture in Romans 10:17 was active in my life.

> "So faith comes from hearing, and hearing through the word of Christ."

I have read enough scripture and heard enough faith-building messages in my life to know that I needed to believe God and not believe in my circumstances. As I sat at my computer researching Sjögren's syndrome and Lupus, I remember turning to my wife and saying, "Honey, we have to be very careful about what we focus on and what we agree with. We cannot enter into despair and doubt." I also told her not to tell people that our son had either of these conditions. If people asked, we would tell them that the doctors are concerned that he might have an autoimmune illness, but God is bigger and He's able to heal Jacob from anything. Through the course of our battle we were determined to never speak negatively of it and we would always speak healing over him. Proverbs 18:21 reads:

> "Death and life are in the power of the tongue, and those who love it will eat its fruits."

Our speech over a circumstance is very important. What we say indicates what we believe and what we expect. What we focus on is always what we will achieve. Ephesians 4:29 instructs us to not let any unwholesome talk come out of our mouths. This verse isn't just talking about curse words and gossip; it also refers to speaking faith versus doubt, life versus death, fear versus confidence. There are two realities happening simultaneously in this world battling for our vote, and whichever one we speak to is the one we will see come to fruition in our lives. The two realities are the visible reality and the faith reality. Visible reality is what we see with our eyes and hear with our ears and whatever is from our other senses. It's the doctor's report, it's the rash we see, it's the wife that leaves for another man, it's the son that's addicted to substances, etc. The typical expected outcome of these situations is what we might focus on. We might say, "Well, I've never seen anyone healed from Lupus, so I can't expect my son to be healed." Or, "I've never seen a marriage restored as bad as mine is." You see what I'm saying? On the other hand, faith reality is what the Word of God says about situations, and is usually in direct opposition to our visible reality. For the child that has Lupus, we know that God is able to heal and His word has much to say about it. For the broken marriage, we know that God's Word says that the heart of a king is in the hand of the Lord (Proverbs 21:1), which means He can transform a husband's or wife's heart, too..

On the day that Jacob was diagnosed with Lupus, we decided something very crucial. We would never speak of the Lupus diagnosis in a defeated way. We would take it to the Lord, we would speak life and healing over our son. We took Jacob to our church's prayer team every week for about 7 weeks. We were blessed to be going to Jesus Culture in Folsom, California; they truly believe in miracles... and see them on a regular basis. We were so encouraged by them and by other stories of healing, particularly one of a man being healed from Lupus. I hung on to those stories as builders of my faith. I also bought an acoustic guitar and we began to sing songs of worship every night in our home. We sang, "Nothing but the blood of Jesus" almost every night. My kids would dance while we worshiped and we filled our house with joy. We were going to be a family like no other, a family worshiping in the darkness, expecting the sunrise.

<u>God knows why</u>

If a bad doctor's report is causing you to battle with fear, it's important to note that a diagnosis is the *doctor's* report, and the *doctor's* words; it's what he or she understands through science, physical exams, lab results, and years of schooling and clinical practice. But we can be "experts" in faith because our hope is found in God's Word, in *His* report. It's God's Word versus the word of man. In regards to my son's diagnosis, in man's finite mind, Lupus and these other illnesses have no known cure because the source of them is still not fully understood. They can be treated, and symptoms can be controlled to a point. Without treatment, Lupus is often fatal and those with the disease often die from kidney failure (source MayoClinic.org).

But God in His infinite mind understands the disease, and I trust He has the knowledge for me to fight it on behalf of my son, both naturally and supernaturally. I can ask the One with infinite knowledge how to fight something man doesn't understand. That is supernatural!

1 Corinthians 2:6 says, "'For who has understood the mind of the Lord so as to instruct him?" But we have the mind of Christ.'" So if we seek God, we can have the mind of the Son of God. That's an amazing thing to grasp.

Here's a story to drive home my point. I used to work as a foreman for a construction company. On one occasion, my boss wanted me to have a try at fixing an ongoing problem in the house of a customer. This problem was with the communications between the home computer system and the air conditioning unit on the 3rd floor. Knowledgeable repairmen had come for years to fix this problem and nobody was able to fix it. My thought was initially, "If experts couldn't fix it, how was I supposed to tackle it?" So I prayed, "God, I don't have any idea what is wrong with this system, but I know YOU DO! Could you please make me aware of what's wrong so I can fix it?" So I began to troubleshoot the problem as I listened closely to the voice of God, telling me to check this and that, and try using this cable detector here and there. Within three hours I had tracked the problem and repaired it before the end of the day. I called my boss to tell him that the problem was fixed. His response was an astounded, "Whoooa!"

While battling for Jacob's healing in prayer, I remembered that occurrence, and thought I would put the same wisdom into practice. Doctors don't really understand Lupus and the actual direct causes, but God does. So I asked Him the same question once again, "God I don't understand what has caused Jacob to have this autoimmune disease and neither do doctors, but I know that you do understand. Could you please show me what to do for my son?" Over the course of the coming weeks, I began to get senses of the things that might have affected my son to cause his body to begin attacking itself. I don't want to get too deep into the things I believe God gave me the wisdom to uncover, because I'm not going to try to be a doctor for others going through autoimmune illnesses. I will say that God began to reveal to me one by one, how various things he was eating and drinking were like poison to him.

So with my spiritual knowledge, I fought the battle daily in prayer supernaturally, speaking life and healing over my son, and the rest of the time I used the wisdom God gave me to fight the disease naturally, as well. Jacob still needed a miracle, however, and the road ahead was still pretty long. We will get back to his story later in the next few chapters, but there are some key ingredients to overcoming that we have to talk about first.

CHAPTER 4

THE WRESTLING MATCH

Have you ever been to a wrestling match? Have you ever seen a wrestler get dressed in his uniform, put on protective head gear, and when the referee blows the whistle for the start of the match, he cowers in the corner screaming, "Leave me alone! Get off of me! Stop it!" Meanwhile he flails his arms like someone defending himself from an attacker far stronger than he is? I bet you've never seen that. But the fact is, that is the way most Christians "fight" everyday battles with the enemy of their souls.

Let me unpack in simple terms a verse that you have probably heard a thousand times, especially if you grew up in church. Ephesians 6:12 says, "For we do not wrestle against flesh and blood, but against the rulers, against the authorities, against the cosmic powers over this present darkness, against the spiritual forces of evil in the heavenly places." I have to admit, I've heard this verse enough times for it to go straight in one ear and out the other. At one point in dealing with my son's diagnosis of Lupus, the prayers that I prayed and spiritual battling that I did on his behalf could have been described as wrestling. I prayed with such tenacity, and rebuked the enemy of sickness with such intensity and force that this verse came to life for me. God showed me the key to this verse, "WE WRESTLE". God spoke to my heart one day and said, "If you're not wrestling, you're not doing the work of the kingdom." If you do not engage the darkness, you're letting it win.

He began to make clear to me that to wrestle is not to fight in a passive defensive stance, just hoping that the enemy will finally leave me alone. Rather it should be an offensive stance in which I pursue the enemy to subdue him. Wrestlers never fight just to get through the match and go home unscathed; they wrestle to subdue an opponent. In a sense, fighting with the attitude of "I'm coming after you, and I'm going to break down your stronghold of sickness with faith and the Word of God." No more running, no more whimpering, no more playing around: just powerful, faith-filled prayer that says "I will not stop until you have been defeated in this particular battle."

It is in this attitude of tenacity that we should approach the battles of our lives. But let's face it – think of a person you know who is going through a struggle. They're probably facing the struggle with tears, dejection, depression and a longing to just make it through. They're probably talking about the problem like it's huge and insurmountable, using phrases like, "I don't know how to make it through", "I don't know what to do", "When will this ever end?" It's time to change that weak, passive stance and stand up! Believe the Word of God! Encourage yourself in the Lord! Wrestle in prayer! Obtain the victory!

> **Wrestlers never fight just to get through the match and go home unscathed. They wrestle to subdue an opponent.**

Victory is a word we need to ponder for a minute. Getting victory in a circumstance implies that there was a battle. There was a wrestling match. When was the last time you wrestled in prayer and believed that you were stronger than your opponent? We who are believers in Christ and have put our faith in Him belong to the kingdom of heaven. "We are seated with Christ in heavenly places," (Ephesians 2:6). We should see all difficulties and battles from the top down. Picture yourself as the larger opponent in the battle, because you truly are. Once you begin to stand on what God's Word says, and begin to pray with the faith of Jacob, who wrestled with the Angel of the Lord refusing to let go until he received a blessing (Genesis 32), you will begin to obtain the victory in the wrestling match. Go after the victory and pursue it until the enemy is defeated in your life and you receive the blessing from God that you so desperately need.

Practically speaking, we can do this by knowing what the Word of God says about our particular circumstance and applying it. When my son's sickness was at its worst and his body was 80-90% covered with lesions and rashes, I would go up to a hilltop at the lake and literally shout victorious scriptures to the sky such as "No weapon that is fashioned against you shall succeed, and you shall refute every tongue that rises against you in judgment. This is the heritage of the servants of the Lord," (Isaiah 54:17). "And with His wounds we are healed," (Isaiah 53:5) I would command the enemy to take his hands off of my son, and simultaneously declare healing over my son according to God's Word. I would remind God of the verses in Exodus that say, "If you will diligently listen to the voice of the Lord your God, and do that which is right in his eyes, and give ear to his commandments and keep all his statutes, I will put none of the diseases on you that I put on the Egyptians, for I am the Lord, your healer," (Exodus 15:26).

That verse brings us to ponder something very important, and we won't spend much time on it. That verse we just read is what I call an "IF, THEN verse". The verse gives you an option. If you do X, God will do Y. The problem is, we can choose not to do X and then God has no obligation to do Y. My point is this: If we want to be able to use scripture to battle with the enemy, we had better make sure our lives are lining up with the verses we are speaking. I can't claim that God will keep me from every disease if I'm not being careful to do what he's commanded. God loves us unconditionally but there are conditions to his blessings, just like there would be conditions in everyday life. If you don't work, you'll go broke. If you smoke too much, you might get lung cancer. Don't do things to harm yourself and you probably won't get hurt. Live recklessly and there is no guarantee.

People who are results driven often have difficulty praying through an issue because prayer is an invisible force, the results of which often seem intangible and slow moving. But the scriptures tell us, "And let us not grow weary of doing good, for in due season we will reap, if we do not give up," (Galatians 6:9). Just like that wrestler doesn't give up easily in a match, you too, should not give up so easily when facing matters too large for yourself.

This next story is about that very thing. It was a matter of praying for something too large for myself, and I wouldn't see the results of the prayers prayed for nearly 4 years. I have a friend named Bill, that I met in 2014. The funny thing is, I've never seen his face in person. We met accidentally when I called the wrong audio visual rental company to rent some microphones. We made a friendship connection for a reason I can't remember, but God wanted it to happen. God knew that Bill was about to enter a crisis and needed support in prayer. Shortly after our meeting on the phone, Bill entered into that crisis. One of the issues was that his son, Paul, was leaving a drug rehabilitation program and was still not on the right path. He was heading back to a life of drugs, and now he was selling drugs. I prayed on the phone with Bill a few times, but I actually prayed for his son constantly in my daily prayer time. I was declaring God's will over his life and commanding Satan to take his hands off of Bill's son. I prayed for him for many months. About a year later, Paul was out doing a drug deal, and he brought his semi-automatic handgun with him. The deal went south and the buyers robbed him, took his gun and put it to his head and pulled the trigger. *Click!* The gun didn't fire because the magazine wasn't pushed all the way in. The men beat him severely, putting him in the hospital. That night, God spared Paul's life because there was still a plan for him, and a father and a friend were praying God's will to be done in his life. That near-death experience almost brought Paul back to his senses and back to a renewed walk with God, but not quite. The battles with drugs, and drug dealing would still last another two and a half years. But the father never gave up praying for his son. I just spoke with Bill a few days ago for an update. Paul reached out to his dad because he had had enough, so the two of them went on a long hiking trip together in Israel. They've reconnected and are together under one roof again. Bill told me that his son has really turned his life around... He is clean. He is sober. He is attending church.

This type of miracle will take a lot of wrestling in prayer to see a breakthrough. The cover of this book says, "No more pulling punches". If you knew that God would answer a prayer after 4 years, would you quit praying at 3 years 11 months? We have given up too easily all our lives when it comes to prayer. I don't know if it's because we don't believe God will answer, or we lack the perseverance, or maybe we think for some reason it's impossible for a situation like that to turn around. If you're facing an insurmountable problem like the story of Bill and his son, let me encourage you to grab someone who will pray with you. I said PRAY with you, not mope with you. There is victory to be won if we will wrestle in prayer. We know what God's will is in these situations. God's Word says that "He is patient toward you, not wishing that any should perish, but that all should reach repentance." (2Peter 3:9) So because we know what God's will is, we can pray with confidence that it is God's desire for the lost son to come home. God desires restoration of relationships. It's why He died on the cross for our sins, so that we might be restored to our original father son/daughter relationship with our Heavenly Father. Therefore we know it's His will to bring the lost son home.

So we wrestle in prayer until we see God's will done. We don't cower in the corner waiting for the attack to end. We stand up and wrestle knowing that we are seated with Christ.

CHAPTER 5

I WENT TO THE ENEMY'S CAMP

In old Pentecostal church circles, there is this old song people used to sing, maybe some still sing it. I've watched people jump up and down with frenzied excitement as they sing a song about going into the enemy's camp and taking back what he stole from them.

I had heard it a hundred times growing up and every time I heard it, I had this giant question mark over my head. I kept asking; "What in the world does this song mean?" I don't think many people in the room ever really understood it. Had anyone in the room really gone to the enemy's camp and taken back what he had stolen from them? Is the enemy really "under their feet" as the song suggests? And if he was, why are they still struggling to overcome so many issues? Perhaps there was one or two in the room who fully grasped the meaning, and had applied it.

In the book of 1 Samuel, the wives, servants, sons and daughters of David and his men had been stolen by the Amalekites when they raided Ziklag, where David and his men were staying. The Amalekites burned the city and stole everything from David and his men. 1 Samuel 30:6 says; "And David was greatly distressed, for the people spoke of stoning him, because all the people were bitter in soul, each for his sons and daughters. But David strengthened himself in the Lord his God." David then inquired of the Lord whether he should go and attack the enemy and take everything back. The answer from God was "Yes". David took six hundred men with him, which diminished to 400 because some became too weary, and David raided the enemy camp and took back all of the people and plunder that the enemy had stolen. God gave them the victory!

> **It's time to encourage yourself in the Lord, and decide to go to the enemy's camp and take back what he stole from you.**

The fact is, the enemy has gone to where you live and stolen from you over and over. Someone in your household is sick continuously. You feel depressed. You struggle each day for joy and you wake up and feel you can't get this "victory" people talk about. It's time to encourage yourself in the Lord, and decide to go to the enemy's camp and take back what he stole from you. That statement, however, is a little too ambiguous and metaphorical to be easily applied, so let's break it down.

Encourage yourself in the Lord. This is covered in depth in the chapter on encouraging yourself, but in simple short terms, we must find the promises of God in the scriptures that apply to our situation. Then we speak those words, find strength in those truths, and trust that God's Word is the reality, not our situation. For example: Have you been given a grim diagnosis from the doctor? God's Word says "He took our illnesses and bore our diseases." Matthew 8:17. His Word also states, "No good thing does he withhold from those who walk uprightly" Psalm 84:11. Is healing a good thing? Yes. Is your walk upright and blameless? That's between you and God, but if the answer is "yes" then you can encourage yourself with this scripture. Don't believe or focus on the negative stories of other people. People who magnify and exalt their failures and unhappy endings will drag you down with their expertise in negativity faster than you can imagine. Simply focus on God's Word and His promises.

Now that you're encouraged, it's time to go fight. Your weapon is prayer and the Word of God. I can't explain to you why prayers do something in the spiritual realm, or why the more I pray for one thing, the more progress seems to happen in that area, I just know that the Word says, "The prayer of a righteous person has great power as it is working." (James 5:16) In some other translations, the word "fervent" is there to describe the prayer. Webster's dictionary defines fervent as: 1. exhibiting or marked by great intensity of feeling : 2. Very hot: So it's time to go pray for that issue you've been facing to be resolved, intensely, fervently, loudly, boldly, incessantly. That is how a battle is fought. It begins to tear down the difficulties and bring God's plan into motion. No wrestler fights with a half-hearted effort unless he plans to lose. No soldier goes into hand-to-hand combat only intending to use half his effort unless he wants to die. So you, too, should go to the enemy's camp to fight with all your strength and fervency. Don't be a wimp about it, this isn't a five minute devotional; it's a battle for your life!

Here's a very simple example of going to the enemy's camp and taking back what he's attempting to steal. Several years ago, while I was worship director in Beaufort SC, one of our team members who sang and played keys was always absent on Sundays for many weeks in a row because she was suffering from migraine headaches. They wouldn't be that bad during the week, but for some reason, every Sunday they would be so severe she couldn't get out of bed. We knew she wasn't faking it because she loved to come be a part of the team.   It seemed to be an obvious play from the enemy to keep her from doing what God had gifted her to do. So I had decided before I got to church that Sunday that if she wasn't there again due to Migraines, I would have her mom, (who was also on the worship team) go and get her from home and bring her so we could pray for her. As I suspected it was the same scenario, so I sent the mother home to get her and bring her so we could pray for her. She returned with her daughter and right before the service, we placed our hands on her head, and I commanded that headache to leave in the name of Jesus and never return. I did as Jesus did in Luke 4:39 when he rebuked the fever. Then I invited God's peace to take over. Her headache left that moment. She was able to join us on the worship team from then on without hindrance. I just spoke with her parents today, (which is 5 years after the event) they said that she's barely had a headache since then except for what any person might occasionally have.

> At that moment, something turned on inside of me. Yes, I was frustrated, but I turned it into a type of praying that would not let go.

In regards to my son's battle with an autoimmune illness, here is how I went to the enemy's camp: I prayed daily for about 8 months, I fasted on two or three occasions, listened to sermons about miracles and healing constantly to gain strength, read the Bible, put my hands on my son's face in the middle of the night declaring healing and scriptures over him, rebuking sickness in the name of Jesus. As the months went by his visual appearance would improve for a while then suddenly stop improving, as if a wall or an impasse was reached in this battle. It happened 3 or more times. And each time I recall in order to get past this wall of sorts, I had to turn up the intensity of prayer, turn up the fervency or heat of the praying. I prayed more often, for longer periods of time, more loudly, speaking more scriptures of healing and

God's promises to answer our prayers. And then in the beginning of April 2016 I noticed that my son's face, which already had lesions and rashes covering both of his cheeks like a beard of red rings, began to get worse. The rings got darker, and I noticed a new mark beginning to grow just underneath his left eye. I had seen this before about 8 months earlier. This was the beginning of a new lesion starting that might take another 6 months to take its course by spreading all over his face before disappearing.

This was the last straw! At that moment, I was so tired of seeing the enemy, in the form of sickness, having any place in my family. At that moment, something turned on inside of me. Yes, I was frustrated, but I turned it into a type of praying that would not let go. At first I was angry with God. My fleshly, human emotion was coming out, but it was doing something that pointed me in the right direction. I said to the Lord in prayer, "God you said 'NO GOOD THING WILL YOU WITHHOLD FROM THOSE WHOSE WALK IS UPRIGHT', so don't withhold this healing from my son and my family!" I recited the parable of the persistent widow to the Lord.

> "God, I want to tell other people someday that you heal sickness. How can I tell others that when my own son is sick?"

> "And he (Jesus) told them a parable to the effect that they ought always to pray and not lose heart. [2] He said, "In a certain city there was a judge who neither feared

> God nor respected man. [3] And there was a widow in that city who kept coming to him and saying, 'Give me justice against my adversary.' [4] For a while he refused, but afterward he said to himself, 'Though I neither fear God nor respect man, [5] yet because this widow keeps bothering me, I will give her justice, so that she will not beat me down by her continual coming.'" [6] And the Lord said, "Hear what the unrighteous judge says. [7] And will not God give justice to his elect, who cry to him day and night? Will he delay long over them? [8] I tell you, he will give justice to them speedily. Nevertheless, when the Son of Man comes, will he find faith on earth?" (Luke 18:1-8)

After reading this, I said "God, if you think that widow was persistent, you haven't seen anything yet. I'm going to be ten times more persistent than that widow, I will not shut up, I will cry out day and night until you heal my son! I will never stop." It may sound bratty and arrogant, but I began to realize this was how God wanted me to pray. It was a determination to stand on God's Word no matter what. It wasn't me telling God what to do, it was God and I partnering to see His Word come to pass. It was true faith. It was in the face of continued disappointment and seemingly unanswered prayers that I continued to pray and believe. I found myself saying, "God, I want to tell other people someday that you heal sickness. How can I tell others that when my own son is sick?"

I ended up for the next 5 days or so crying out to God like this five to six times a day. I was yelling at the top of my lungs, "God heal my son! I'm not going to shut up until it's done! God, you said 'No good thing will you withhold from those whose walk is upright.' Don't withhold this healing from my son." I continued to quote scriptures that support healing and God doing miracles. I was on a mission like never before, battling in prayer in the enemy's camp with God at my side.

You'll have to wait until one of the following chapters to find out what happened next. Before I get to that there are still a few more lessons to learn about this process of victory.

CHAPTER 6

ENCOURAGE YOURSELF

Have you ever received an encouraging phone call from someone while in a deep, dark place in your life that just lifted your spirits? It probably did the job of making you feel better, but only until the next day when you woke up still in the middle of your struggle, and feeling discouraged. At least that's how it was for me for a long time. Many of us look to someone close to lift us up when we face problems or feel down in the dumps. And if after talking to that person we don't feel encouraged enough, we move on to the next person who can make us feel better. While I am an advocate of surrounding yourself with encouraging people, the encouragement you receive from other people only lasts for a few moments. God's encouragement from His Word is permanent if we grab hold of it and believe it.

Something life changing happened during one of my prayer times just after my son was diagnosed with his autoimmune illness. I would often go to a secluded part of a lake to pray each day for quite some time. This particular time, I was holding back tears as I began to seek God for the healing of my son. As I was talking with God, I said out loud, "God, you've got to encourage me! I need your encouragement." Immediately I heard a sentence very, very clearly in my heart, a sentence that I knew couldn't be me because this type of thought had never crossed my mind. It was the voice of God's spirit speaking to me. "Steve, encourage yourself." I was shocked. Here I was asking my Father in heaven to encourage me like I needed, and He's telling me to do it myself. I responded out loud, "What do you mean, encourage myself?" The inner voice responded. "Steve, you already know everything my Word has to say about healing and my promises to you. Now go find them, read them, and speak them back to me." I didn't fully understand the lesson that was about to take place, but I listened to and heeded that word. I opened the Bible on my phone and began to search out each verse in the Bible that had a promise to me and my family regarding healing, hope, abundant life and every good thing God has prepared for those who love him. I began to speak those verses out loud to God, telling him that I understood that his promises are for health for my son and not to have a chronic disease. I won't spell out all the verses. There are too many. As I spoke these verses out with confidence to God, the discouragement subsided, in fact, it turned into downright joyful hope. In a matter of a few moments my disposition changed simply by reading aloud God's promises back to Him. I felt like God and I were in this together, like He was by my side saying, "We are going to win this battle together."

While that is a pretty cool thing that happened, the more important thing was that the encouragement I received that day never subsided. I woke up every day encouraged and with hope, not in depression or despair over my son's health. I did have to return to that place of quoting scripture many times over the course of the battle, but I didn't need other people to do it for me. Unlike other people's encouraging words, God's encouragement from His Word is permanent if we grab hold of it and believe it, just like David did.

Learning to encourage yourself by knowing who God is, and what He has said about your circumstance in the Bible will get you through many trials when you are alone, or when nobody seems to be of any help or encouragement to you at all. I believe this is the way God designed it. He wanted our understanding of who he is to guide our emotions and expectations in every situation (good or bad) in our lives. He has said that you can do all things through Christ who gives you strength. (Philippians 4:13) He has said that He is the God who forgives all your sins and heals all your diseases. (Psalm 103:3) He has said that He would not withhold any good thing from those who's walk is upright and blameless. (Psalm 84:11) We are not to be pressed down and defeated by the attack of the enemy because we are actually seated with Christ in heavenly places. (Ephesians 2:6) He said that He knows exactly how you feel because he experienced all the pressure that you have faced as well. (Hebrews 4:15)

I could go on forever, but the ultimate point of

encouraging yourself is this: You have to know what the Bible says so that you can combat the lies the enemy speaks to you. The enemy's lies are what discourage you. So knowing the Bible and speaking back the truth is the first key of going from discouragement to joy. I was always taught that you combat lies with the truth. But God's truth is invisible until we activate it with faith. Whatever we believe is what we focus on. One final story to bring this point home. The evidence I saw everyday in my son's face, said that he had a severe illness that to my knowledge, nobody had ever been cured from before. That's the visible evidence. The lie is "Nobody else has been healed from this, neither will your son be healed." The truth of God's word is in short, God will not withhold healing from those who's walk is upright , because healing is a good thing and God doesn't withhold good things from his children who love Him and obey Him. So I begin to focus on the unseen truth rather than the visible lie, and in doing so I begin to be encouraged. Hey guys, it's not easy, and it takes effort just like going on a diet or starting an exercise program, but it will bring the results to take you to a place of victory and joy.

CHAPTER 7

MEDS FOR ANXIETY AND DEPRESSION?

I was breathing rapidly, but felt like no air was coming into my lungs. My heart was racing above 120 bpm; I got out of bed in a panic, but couldn't even walk straight.

Unfortunately, night terrors were a normal part of my childhood. I can remember being in bed with my parents, having nightmares from which I just couldn't wake up. They were absolutely paralyzing; everything moving or stationary was a sinister monster. The dresser drawers were moving, the walls were crawling, even my mom's face looked frightening. "Stephen....Look at me, look at me, wake up!" My mom would continually call to me. But I would suffer in terror for what felt like hours at a time, and it probably was hours. I was unable to wake up, unable to shake the fear. This went on for years. I wish I understood then what I understand now about spiritual battles and fighting fear. If my parents only understood what I do now, they would have taken an offensive stance against this fear, just like I do now whenever it arises.

Fear is not just something that happens inside your mind, I'm convinced it can also be external from evil spiritual forces, and the methods for fighting those forces should likewise be spiritual. 2 Corinthians 10:4-5 states "For the weapons of our warfare are not of the flesh, but have divine power to destroy strongholds. [5] We destroy arguments and every lofty opinion raised against the knowledge of God" The Word of God is a powerful weapon to fight fear, anxiety, depression and all kinds of negative thoughts and emotions, especially when it's spoken out loud.

Night terrors weren't only isolated to my childhood. They stopped for a number of years, but would you believe that they returned when I was 40 years old? I was in the middle of the battle for my son's healing. I was lying in bed one night asleep, and I suddenly was awakened with the similar feeling I had when I was just a little boy, except this time, I literally feared for my life. I felt like I was suffocating to death, mixed with the similar fear from childhood. Once again, I couldn't fully wake up, I was trapped in this mode of terror. I was breathing rapidly but felt like no air was coming in my lungs, my heart was racing above 120 bpm; I got out of bed in a panic, but couldn't even walk straight. My legs were like jello beneath me. My voice was trembling and my hands were shaking uncontrollably. It was so severe that I was ready to call 911, but first I called a friend on the other side of the country at 4am and asked him to pray with me. He prayed with me and I began to quote scripture over myself. I read Psalm 91: "I will not fear the terror of night nor the arrow that flies by day". I just kept quoting that scripture and sang songs of worship. But I began to notice something I never experienced before. Only quoting God's word had any effect against this fear. I listened to worship music and it hardly helped. I prayed and it seemed to have little effect, but the more scripture I quoted the more the fear would subside. I tried to go back to bed, but the fear and shaking would return, so I quoted scriptures again until the fear would go away. I suffered from this type of irrational fear for about a month, and every time I battled it with scripture. I believe I was going through this because of the intensity of the battle I was in for my son's healing. I was at war with darkness, and it was at war with me. I would memorize verses and tell myself before bed which scriptures to quote if I was confronted with terror in the middle of the night. I battled this way for weeks until the fear was gone, and since that month of battling it hasn't returned. What I didn't know about this experience, I learned a few weeks later when talking with a friend. His wife suffers daily from the same type of irrational fear. I guess they call them "panic attacks" and it's often treated with anti-anxiety and anti-depression medications. The title of this chapter "Medication for anxiety and depression?" is meant for you to ask yourself a question. Please don't be offended, but have you tried the scripture or prayer method for what you're facing, or have you simply begun to rely on medication?

The Bible says that we can be transformed by the renewing of our minds. (Romans 12:2) Also in 1 Corinthians 2:16, it states that we have the mind of Christ. In addition we are instructed in 2 Corinthians 10:5 to " take every thought captive to obey Christ". I don't know how many scriptures

> **Thus far in my life I've found one sure fire method for dealing with anxiety and depression, and that method is simply time spent with Jesus.**

people need to hear to begin to believe that there is a point our Father in Heaven is trying to make, but for me three scriptures is enough. I know that mental battles can be won with the Word of God. It's not always easy or immediate, but in my experience it is much more thorough and complete than medication. Jesus went through this same fear and anxiety. He was so filled with fear and anxiety that He sweat blood at the thought of carrying the sins of the world and dying on the cross. He's familiar with human emotions and the mind, and he's made a way through our relationship with God to have peace and to overcome anxiety.

Let me give you one more example. I believe that creative people suffer from depression more frequently than non-creatives. Artists, comedians, painters, and all those who express what's inside of them through some sort of art, usually have one thing in common: a desire to live with purpose, and for people to be affected positively by their work. I'm no different. My heart burns inside of me to make a difference through the work of my hands, or through expression through media and even with this book that I'm writing. No one wants his or her work to go unnoticed or to be ineffectual. Many days I wake up with feelings of inadequacy or the fear that my work will never amount to anything memorable. Sometimes these feelings cross the border into depression. Thus far in my life I've found one sure fire method for dealing with it, and that method is simply time spent with Jesus. Each morning I have to do exactly what those verses say, "..take every thought captive" and bring it to submission of Christ. I have to "...renew my mind" daily through prayer and listening to God's word. I have to speak His promises over my life every day. Finally, each day after doing this, the depression leaves and I can return to a joyful disposition ready to face each day with joy and hope. Like I said, it's not always easy, because it takes discipline to do that. It's so much easier to simply take pills that change the chemical balance and cause you to "feel normal". But we know that pills don't provide lasting results; only the peace of God living inside of you can do that. Only Jesus can take the anxiety and negative emotions and replace them with His peace and promises. It just takes our focus to believe what He says to us, that He has a plan for us to prosper us and give us a hope and a future (Jeremiah 29:11).

I know that there are people reading this right now

saying, "But you don't know the depths of my depression and anxiety." Correct, I don't know, but I know the depths of what I face daily, and I can confidently say that without time with Jesus, it's much much worse. Time in the Word, declaring it's truth over your life, and actively coming against the lies from the enemy is our shield of faith that extinguishes those fiery darts. This is what can conquer depression and anxiety. Since the beginning of time, there has been power for you to tap into to overcome negative emotions. Jesus knows how you feel and He has made a way for you to overcome and conquer.

CHAPTER 8

WHY IS IT TAKING SO LONG?

I know that in previous chapters, the answers to prayer that I mentioned seemed to happen fairly quickly in most cases. But what if it takes a really long time before you see an answer to your prayer? What if you've been praying for years to see any hope of getting out of that desert? Aside from praying for more than 8 months to see an answer in my son's case, I do have another example of a miracle happening at the end of a long road.

The house my wife and I bought a couple years after getting married was a town house. The walls on either side of the house were attached to someone else's town house. This was not really an issue initially. But we had neighbors that smoked nearly four packs a day between the two of them. At first their rule for themselves was only to smoke outside, so the smoke would usually blow off into infinity. Going outside in the backyard to play with our kids was usually not a good idea because their smoke would go over the courtyard wall and just sit in ours. So if we decided to play outside with the kids, we'd get a heavy dose of nicotine. After a few years they decided to take their habit indoors, as well as outdoors. Then they added marijuana to their repertoire. We found out soon that there were invisible passageways and porous areas where smoke from the neighbors would end up in our house. Countless mornings we would wake up with cigarette smoke in our home. On top of the constant wheezing in my chest, my wife and I were concerned for the health of our two sons. The problem went from bad to worse each month as the permanent smell of smoke got thicker and thicker and the smell of marijuana would greet us at the door. We purchased the most expensive air purifiers and charcoal filters, but their effects were not lasting. Selling the house became an impossible concept. Who would buy a house from which the obvious smell of cigarettes and marijuana greeted you with a punch at the door? I didn't know what to do. We couldn't sell the house. Who would want to rent it from us?

I began to pray each day for rescuing from this current situation. If I would make a movie clip to illustrate this example of ongoing prayer, I might show a family praying at a table wearing winter clothes and decorating the house for Christmas. Then the scene would fade to kids playing outside in the springtime, then fade back to the family praying again at a birthday party for their son, followed by the family dressed in summer clothes praying again in the same location around the dinner table. More birthdays, holidays and seasons would pass while the children look older in each scene. The fact is, that's what happened in our lives. Years passed with this situation of breathing in smoke every day.

Then one day...

I got a phone call from a previous client whose name was Rob. I had taken aerial and interior video of his house a few years back when he originally put it on the market for sale. It was a beautiful, two story, 3600 square foot home on the banks of a beautiful river, priced at over 1 million dollars. In South Carolina a 1 million dollar house would be the equivalent of a two or three million dollar house in west coast cities. His house also had a half Olympic lap pool in the backyard and a 500 foot boat dock. The client was requesting photos I shot of the house 2 years back because he was going to list it with another agency. The problem was, I never shot any photos, just video. So I let him know I didn't have any photos of his house, but he kept persisting that I had photos. I heard the voice of the Holy Spirit say to me, "Don't blow him off". So I called him back and said, "I don't have any photos of your house, but I'd be happy to come over and take some photos." So I went over to Rob's house that afternoon to take photos of the interior and exterior, and then spent some time with him until it was dark so I could take night pictures of the pool and exterior lighting. During some down time, he began to share with me. "It's a shame that nobody is ever here to use this beautiful pool." he said. "You know, I could give you a key to the house and you and your wife and kids could come over and use it anytime you wanted." I was taken aback by the generous offer, and began to wonder if this was perhaps going to be the answer to our prayers to get out of our smoke-filled house... but it seemed too wonderful to even imagine. We talked a little longer and Rob paid me twice what I asked him for the photos and I went home.

About a week or so passed by and I felt impressed by God to send Rob an email asking him how much he was hoping to rent the house for during the sale process. He replied saying that he was hoping for $5000/mo. Needless to say I was in no position to pay this much for rent on a house that I considered a mansion. I was too embarrassed to respond with my initial thought – "Wow, that's a lot!" So I said that I would get back to him. Rob was in Texas for business so I decided that my family and I should take a drive over to his house to look at it and pray. We pulled into the long, curved driveway amidst a beautifully manicured front lawn. My kids got out and marveled at the size of the house and the awesomeness of the view. We prayed together as a family that God would use this house to help us out of our current situation and then we left. Looking back, it seems crazy to think that we would have had that kind of faith to believe that an answer to that prayer would be possible, but we really did believe.

A few days later, once again I felt impressed by the Holy Spirit to send a very specific email to Rob. Here's the actual text from the email:

> *"How is that job search going? I read that email that said you had your name in for a position. How's it looking?*

> I just wanted to let you know that after some number crunching I've come to the conclusion that I couldn't offer you a reasonable amount to rent your house. I just don't have the income. That's not to say that we wouldn't take great care of your home. But we wouldn't even put a dent in your monthly expenses to keep that house. Thank you for offering the pool to use. It's very kind. We do plan on taking you up on that offer, but it's been raining here like crazy. Much of Beaufort was flooded last night. Let me know how your job search is going. I'm still lifting you up in prayer. May God bless you with a job and exceeding joy."

That same day while my wife and I were driving to church, I received an email from Rob. When I opened it and began to read, I literally shouted for joy at what he said. Here's an excerpt from that email:

> "...finally, I need someone to live in the house (for ins. and practical reasons) even if they don't pay much or any rent, until I decide what to do with it. Would you be interested? you'd have to move in your furniture of course. My sister has a key to let you in. Once in the house there are some extra door keys(I think) in the top drawer just to the left of the knee hole in the side counter top and you can keep one."

The answer to our years of prayer finally came! Such a long wait, but God rescued us. We moved into that huge house the same week, and entered into what we felt like was finally, a season of peace.

But why did it take so long? There are a number of reasons why the answer to a prayer could take a long time to surface. What I'm about to offer is knowledge gained from a mixture of answered prayers in my own life and the answered prayers of particular people in the

Bible. The first thing I'd like to note is that sometimes the answer to a prayer requires our own obedience to what God is telling us to do. If we stall or don't believe, then we stall that answer to prayer. In this case of the house being provided, I had to be aware of God telling me not to blow off Rob in his request for the photos. That step was critical because it started the whole process. In addition, I had to be willing to believe that God would provide the answer in such an abundant way. Also, I had to be open to the voice of the Holy Spirit speaking about sending those emails. All of these elements which led to the answered prayer were founded in my close relationship with my Father in heaven because every day I spent so much time in prayer seeking Him. The house was never going to fall out of the sky, but God would give a divine strategy for seeing His purpose come about on earth. Another reason it could take a long time to be answered is that the events and circumstances need to be set up by God in advance to see things go from the supernatural to the natural. Rob needed to come to a point that he was willing to even offer what he did. Two years of seeing no results with the sale of his home led him to a place of being willing to offer us his house for little to no rent. It was simply a matter of timing.

Let's look at an example from the Bible about a prayer taking some time. There's one very common example cited about a barrier to answered prayer, and that's the account of Daniel (when he fasted). In Daniel chapter 10, Daniel fasted from good tasting foods and from meat and wine for a period of 21 days. He was visited by an angel in a dream on the 24th day of the month.

The angel's message was that his prayer was heard on the first day, but the angel was prevented from bringing him the answer because of a battle happening in the supernatural realm. Here we see a supernatural delay to an answer to prayer. Perhaps there is a supernatural battle going on which is preventing the answer to your prayer. Our job is to keep pressing in like the persistent widow in Luke 18:1-8, who wouldn't take no for an answer. She needed justice and her persistence finally paid off. I feel I need to mention one thing to help set some of you free. That parable teaches us a very specific message: to pray and never give up, and to be persistent with our prayers. Some teachers and preachers have erroneously stated, "pray about something once, then leave it at the altar. If you pray about it again it means that you don't really have faith." I'm not sure what seminary or Bible school these teachers went to, but that message is counterproductive to what God's word says. We are supposed to pray without ceasing, and we are supposed to be persistent with the same prayers. Jesus himself told the parable about the persistent widow, so I'm confident we can put that into practice.

One final reason I'll share that some prayers may take awhile to be answered, is simply, God is utilizing this circumstance to bring about the best in you and to make you stronger. Quick answers to prayer don't always lead to character development. Sometimes quick answers are necessary, and sometimes God can use the situation for your ultimate good and the good of the body of believers. One example is in Luke 22 when Jesus is talking to Simon Peter just before Jesus is betrayed. Jesus says to him in verse 31

> "Simon, Simon, behold, Satan demanded to have you, that he might sift you like wheat, 32 but I have prayed for you that your faith may not fail. And when you have turned again, strengthen your brothers."

First of all we see that the instigator of the difficulty is Satan, it is not God. But through this sifting, when Simon Peter turns back (or overcomes) then he can encourage the other brothers.

Through my battle of praying for a miracle for my son, I grew so much stronger in my faith. Now I have a reason to write this book to encourage other believers. God did not make my son sick, but he utilized the difficulty to bring about something amazing in my family. It's a testimony that I tell everywhere I go, and people come to Christ and are also healed because of it. I did not like being in the middle of the difficulty, nor do I want to ever go back, but I would not ever trade what was given to us in the process, which was an overcoming spirit. This overcoming spirit could not be cultivated in a day or a week. It took a year of intense pressure, prayer and faith-building determination to never give up believing that God has heard us and His Word is true. Here we stand on the other side of the desert. Let me encourage you to keep praying, being persistent, and growing in your faith and you will come out on the other side with a whole new perspective on life, faith and miracles.

CHAPTER 9

PRAY FOR THE IMPROBABLE

In 2012 through 2014 California went through a very dry spell. California's 2013-2014 rainfall was the worst with only 7.38 inches in the entire year (15.13 inches below average). It was the driest calendar year on record. (www.*ncdc.noaa.gov/sotc/national/201313*) We moved to Folsom, California in April of 2015, and the levels of Folsom Lake, which is one of California's largest reservoirs, were pretty low. I knew that one of my tasks when moving here was to pray for rain for California. I felt it was imperative that people of faith pray for the impossible, even for the ending of a long-lasting drought. I went to the lake almost daily and prayed for God to send rain. I prayed for the water to flow in and fill the lake to the top. I began to build a stone memorial there. I wanted to remember the place where I prayed. I prayed that the stone monument would be covered with water. My kids would also come out to the lake with me and pray for rain. We would gather around the stone monument and pray together as a family. I was teaching my children to pray for the impossible and not be limited in their understanding of God's power to answer prayer. I kept thinking of Elijah praying for rain in the book of 1 Kings 18. I wasn't sure if I was nuts believing that this prayer would have an effect on the situation. I prayed through the fall and into the summer. Not a drop of rain fell. Then one afternoon a thunderstorm came with such a deluge that people were literally kayaking in the streets in one neighborhood. It was only a flash flood and was barely a drop in the bucket compared to what was needed in all of California. After that one rainfall, months went by without a drop of rain falling, but I kept praying. By the end of the summer, Folsom Lake's levels were so low, you could walk out to the middle of the lake where the water would be 100 feet deep if the reservoir were full. The old, inundated town of Mormon Island was visible and you could see ruins of houses and many artifacts from before the time Folsom Lake was a reservoir. But I kept praying.

Believe God for the impossible, the improbable and the unlikely.

Perhaps you know the story already. That winter of 2015-2016, it rained so much, it was the 3rd wettest winter on record. And if that wasn't amazing enough, the next winter of 2016-2017 was the wettest winter since records began being kept. In places in the mountains it snowed more than 29 feet, holding a storehouse of water that would take all the way through 2017 to melt. Folsom Lake was so full that they had to let water out of the reservoir at a rate of more than 60,000 cubic feet per second to prevent flooding. The quiet American River flowing through Folsom, that normally is so calm your child could swim in it, turned into raging rapids flowing 40 miles per hour. The town of Oroville, California was at risk of its dam breaking because of the massive surge of snow melting. People were evacuated for a period of time, but thankfully, the dam held.

I was reluctant to write this story because I didn't want people to think I'm saying that it's because of my prayers that this amazing turn of events took place. I do know that many others were praying, too. My point in telling this story is to believe God for the impossible, the improbable and the unlikely. That's the way all the men of God in the Bible (whose prayers were notably written down) prayed. They were bold, praying for the sun to stand still. (Joshua 10) Marching around Jericho so that the walls would fall. (Joshua 5) Telling the lame man to get up and walk (Acts 3:1) – and the list goes on.

My kids were understanding it, too. My son Jacob said to me one day. "Dad, it hasn't rained in a while. Did you stop praying?" He was right. I had stopped praying.

I remember one time during the beginning of my prayer journey when I just started seeing frequent answers to prayer. It was a Wednesday at our church and a huge community outreach event was planned. We had so many things planned for that Wednesday night, all of it outside. People were coming from all over the community to attend this event. About an hour before the event an absolutely massive thunderstorm was heading down from Charleston straight towards Beaufort. On the radar it was one of the largest thunderstorms I had ever seen. Its arrival in Beaufort was going to be pretty much the same time as the start of the event. What I did next was the boldest thing I had ever done in my prayer life up until that point. I remembered the story in Mark 4:35-40:

> "On that day, when evening had come, he (Jesus) said to them, "Let us go across to the other side." 36 And leaving the crowd, they took him with them in the boat, just as he was. And other boats were with him 37 And a great windstorm arose, and the waves were breaking into the boat, so that the boat was already filling. 38 But he was in the stern, asleep on the cushion. And they woke him and said to him, "Teacher, do you not care that we are perishing?" 39 And he awoke and rebuked the wind and said to the sea, "Peace! Be still!" And the wind ceased, and there was a great calm. 40 He said to them, "Why are you so afraid? Have you still no faith?"

After having spent so many hours in God's presence the past several months, my faith that I could do the same things Jesus did was pretty high. After all Jesus said in Matthew 17:20:

> "For truly, I say to you, if you have faith like a grain of mustard seed, you will say to this mountain, 'Move from here to there,' and it will move, and nothing will be impossible for you."

So I stood outside the church looking at the huge storm that was coming towards us, pointed at it and shouted: "In the name of Jesus you will not come this way, I tell you storm to turn towards the ocean right now." I think I said it at least two or three times. Jesus probably needed only once, however. The funny thing was, I found out later that at the same exact time, our youth pastor was standing on the opposite side of the parking lot doing the exact same thing. I pulled out my weather app on my phone for the next 15 minutes and watched something unbelievable. The storm, which was originally making a beeline straight for our church, made a sudden 90° turn to the east and went out over the ocean. All we received at the church was a beautiful sun shower just before the event. Hundreds of new people came to the church that night for our community outreach. It couldn't have been more beautiful. So am I saying that when you know Jesus that much and operate according to the authority Jesus says we have in Him, we can tell storms to move and they will? Yes, I am.   All of the answers to prayer that I've seen in the past 6 years were all originally prayed because I took Jesus at his Word. I didn't turn his words into metaphors because they didn't make sense. I sought to believe them and understand them and put them into practice, which is why I'm able to tell you to pray for the impossible, the improbable and the unlikely and watch what happens.

CHAPTER 10

WHAT IF IT JUST WON'T BREAK THROUGH?

This is the tough chapter. How do we explain to our family, and even to ourselves, when the answer just won't seem to come? What do you do when you're up against the wall and time has almost run out and nothing seems to work? I don't know about every situation, but I can share with you what we discovered when that happened to our family. It was about six months after we moved into our miracle mansion, you know, the big house that Rob let us live in nearly rent free. I had resigned from my full time job about 8 months earlier and I was running my video business full time. That business was our only source of income, and things were slowing down. Some clients took up to 60 days to pay, another business venture that I started with a friend was failing, and new video business was far too infrequent. All of these elements are not conducive to a stable income, and our money was running out. The fact of the matter was, there just wasn't enough clientele in the area to run a business like mine. After several months our finances started to dwindle, I mean like couldn't-buy-groceries kind of dwindling finances. Our very good friends knew of the situation we were in. They were there walking through it with us, praying for us, with us, counseling us, crying with us. On more than one occasion, they gave us money to get through the month. I kept praying like I always had, declaring success over my business and asking God for supernatural intervention. but for some reason the answers just weren't coming. It used to be that God would send an answer right away in my business enabling me to take care of my family, but for some unknown reason nothing was "working". To make matters way worse, Rob emailed (the following January) to let us know that he was moving back from Texas and would need us out of his house in less than 30 days. We didn't have enough money for a deposit on a rental, and our smoke-filled house was currently being rented out, so we couldn't go back there either. We were out of money, out of food, out of options and about to be out of a place to live.

The next Sunday I went to church and a guest speaker, Joe Phillips was speaking and praying for people after the service. We knew him and decided to go up to him after the service to tell him our problem and ask for prayer. After he listened to our situation he said to me. "I know what it's like to be a dad and to be very fearful of being able to take care of your family." He went on to say that he had no advice for the situation, but he once was in a similar place of desperation. He instructed me to listen to a sermon from a well known speaker, T.D. Jakes, about getting out of your nest. I went home and immediately listened to it. In the message T.D. Jakes spoke on times in which it seemed that nothing you did was working. You couldn't pray your way out of a situation, you could't fast your way out, you couldn't declare your way out, you couldn't rebuke your way out. It's in those times that God is most likely pushing you out of the nest. He's instructing you that it's time to stop relying on your old way of thinking and living.

> **One of the biggest hindrances to many people's faith and growth, is the incorrect thinking that God does everything for you.**

Perhaps it's time to step out in faith in a whole new way that would never happen if you were comfortably taken care of in your current situation. Every species of bird that has to learn to fly, one day needs to leave the nest and try to fly. And a good mother bird will coax the chick to get out of the nest. No more mama bird bringing the worm to you, it's time for you to go get the worm yourself.

That brings me to one very quick point that I already mentioned above: one of the biggest hindrances to many peoples' faith and growth is the incorrect thinking that God does everything for you. As a father, I do things for my kids and provide for them without them having to do anything, that is until they start to grow up and have understanding. Then I expect them to take the knowledge I've given them and begin to do things on their own, to accomplish tasks without much help from me. If my son says, "I can't do it...You do it." My response is "No, God gave you the same brain as me and I'm teaching you how to use it." God is the same way with us because He is a good father.

As I listened to this sermon about getting out of the nest, I remembered a vivid dream I had several years back. It was a dream that I held onto very strongly because in the dream God was clearly marking a path for me to move to California. In those years I even asked myself and my wife, "What kind of circumstance would actually be the catalyst for me packing all our belongings, uprooting my family and driving 3000 plus miles from South Carolina to California? How strong would my faith have to be that this was really what I was supposed to do?"

This was it. All of these struggles and nothing working out was God pushing me out of the nest, out of my comfortable place of living in South Carolina. He was pushing me to go to the place he had instructed me to go years back, and only becoming so destitute and empty in my current location would cause me to actually make this move. Suddenly everything was clear. It was time to move to California to fulfill whatever calling He had for us there.

To prevent us from actually having to live in our van or in someone's basement, which was an impending possibility, I bought a pretty inexpensive RV with the last bit of credit I had. I was making enough money from online sales each month to cover the monthly payment and some groceries and gas. So that's what we did. When we left Rob's house, we moved our stuff to a storage facility and moved into the RV. My 6 month pregnant wife, Jenny, my two sons and my mother in law, crammed in the 2001 Ford RV that we parked in relatives' and friends' driveways. The first night in the RV, the temperature dropped to below freezing. It was a lot of fun actually – more like camping. "We could stand this for a while," I thought. We stayed a few nights outside our friend's house, then a few weeks outside my dad's house making preparations to move to California. Altogether we lived in that RV about 6 weeks.

So what is the answer to the question. "What if it just won't break through?" Perhaps God is speaking to you about something and you're just not hearing it yet, because what he's saying is so profound that it takes your life being shaken up just so you can hear it. Yes, He is being a good father by pushing you out of the nest. He is being a good father by shaking up your life to get you to grow. The answer to your prayers is coming in a way you never ever expected, but you aren't in the right place to receive the answer yet. Receiving the answer in your current place would be a detriment to you. So God is shaking things up.

Maybe you want to know how it turned out? How did the crazy faith move across the country pan out? Well for starters, people thought we were nuts (including family). But after two short months in California we were stable and in an apartment, and I was working as an editor and director of photography for a national PBS television show. This was an opportunity definitely not offered in South Carolina.   After that contract I became a full time media director at one of the largest churches in Sacramento, where I learned much more about live production and team building. I've filmed for several Jesus Culture albums as well as for Chris McClarney.   I'm writing this chapter 2 years and 9 months after moving to California. I'm currently running my video production company, and an online business. We have never thrived so much as we are right now. God is opening doors everywhere we go. Looking back, I would not want my original prayers answered for provision and business where we were 3 years ago, because that would mean we would miss out on the greater blessing after having learned to fly.

CHAPTER 11

TRUST GOD'S GOT YOU

Stepping back in time a little bit, there are some lessons to be learned from our legendary 2,764 mile faith move across the country in our RV. Namely that when you're obedient to God's calling, and are willing to step out, you can be confident that God's got you covered.

Before we left Beaufort, South Carolina, our friends, family, and church family threw us a going away party. We had been part of Praise Assembly for 10 years and had passionately served there. At the party we were given many going away gifts, including about $1000 in gas cards to feed the gas-hungry V10 engine of the Ford RV towing our van. About 6 days into our journey, we hit some wind storms in the plains of Oklahoma and New Mexico. Winds blew straight down the highway against us at 50 mph, which means if we were traveling at 50 mph, the wind resistance made it the same as driving 100 mph. I had the gas pedal planted on the floor and we couldn't break 55 mph. We were thrown back and forth on the highway so much that steering was like a gym workout on biceps day. We were going through $100 gas cards like water, getting about 3 miles per gallon on those two days of heavy wind.

Just before going to sleep that night I made an assessment of our finances and realized that we were just about out of gas money. We could make it just a few hundred miles then we'd be totally out. Remember that what caused us to make this move was that my business had failed where I was, so really all we had was the gas cards and the little bit of online sales income each month. We didn't have a lot to go on starting out. That night I remember that I didn't freak out… I just didn't know what we were going to do. As I laid down on the queen bed in the RV next to my sleeping 6 year old and my wife, I just simply prayed for God to help us, then I fell into a peaceful sleep. Close to midnight, I was awakened by the Facebook Messenger notification on my phone. I picked up the phone and noticed that my friend Kevin Lim from Singapore, a friend I hadn't seen in almost 18 years, messaged me. His message said:

> *"Dude, Saw your video about you traveling in New Mexico, you're maybe like Abraham or something, going to a place only revealed a step at a time. Anyway, it's also good to get practical – is there a way to wire some $$ to you or something? Contribution to your journey…let me know."*

I returned his message and asked him if he could PayPal us some gas money. I had a PayPal debit card so I would have immediate access to any money he sent. He sent us $200, which was enough for another day of traveling.

Now if you don't believe in God, or you don't believe that he is active in the life of someone who prays daily after reading that, then what happened two days later might help.

On April 27th we were in the exact same situation again: out of gas and out of money. We were sitting in the RV at the end of another day of travel when once again my messenger app sounded an alert. The message was from Elena – somebody I had only met once in my life (at my step brother's funeral). This was her message:

> *"I know it's very late but I would like to send you something to help you with your trip. The Spirit told me to do it days ago and I got so wrapped up with work and didn't listen. Please send me a way to be able to send you a little something. You and your family in that short time we met, (I saw) really a life of "Christ's Presence" with you...I am awed by your light that shines..the whole family's light. Be safe traveling and please send me a way I can transfer fund directly to your account (if it makes it easier)."*

I was astounded. Twice in one week God was leading someone to help us. We didn't tell anyone that we were short on gas money, yet God who knew our needs was telling people for us. So basically, the first day we had the trouble with running out of gas, the Spirit of God was already speaking to somebody about it, a person we met only one time! But if you notice something about the people in all these stories, the answers to the prayers came through them. They all heard the voice of God, which meant they were listening. Just like the story of needing the resources for the medical trip to the Philippines, when Scott heard God's voice to write me a check. I believe we all need to come to a place in which we know that God has our needs in mind, and when we pray, we know that he is already making a way. He will probably use a person to be the answer to a prayer and he probably wants you to be an answer to someone else's prayer. The key in all of this is an active daily prayer life. Constant speaking with the Father in heaven makes you aware of His voice, and able to hear his voice through all the noise of this life. Even as I sit here writing this book, we are approaching a potentially difficult place, but these stories remind me that God already has the answer for us and I can trust Him. It doesn't mean that I don't continue to pray and ask. The parable of the persistent widow mentioned earlier in this book tells me to keep asking, and I can pray with confidence that he will make a way.

We have to come to a confident place in our lives that we can really say we trust God. If we don't learn to rest in the trust that he loves us and does have our needs in mind, we can end up in a place of constant stress. I had the opportunity to preach to a Wednesday night church group once. In this message I said that it's time to stop praying for our electric bill to be paid and begin to pray for kingdom principles to be active in our lives. If we are always focused on the lack, and the next bill that is pending, then the answered prayers mean nothing. We haven't realized a place of trust in God yet, so as soon as the prayer for this bill is answered, we're stressed again within a few hours about the next bill. What's the point if you're always stressed and doubting? But when you enter a place of trust, you can be confident that the answer will come, and you can remain in a place of peace. The one thing that no man can give you, no money can buy, and only God can provide to you is PEACE. Proverbs 17:1 says it best. "Better a dry crust with peace and quiet than a house full of feasting, with turmoil."

Our family used to be in a continuous place where we had very little in our bank account (partially because of poor money management) and there was always stress regarding the next bill. Then I've also been in a place where there was plenty of money in the bank, and guess what – I was still stressed about bills that weren't even due for three more months. My problem wasn't our income or how big our bank account was. My problem was trust. I needed to rest in God realizing that He had our backs all along. Psalm 37:25 says, "I was young and now I am old. Yet I have never seen the godly abandoned or their children begging for bread." Likewise, I'm 42 and I haven't starved to death yet, and neither have my kids… and I have 4 of them to feed in California! Even when the woman in our church called me, crying hysterically after she had come home from work to find all her belongings on the ground because she had been evicted – God still had her needs in mind. We took her and her son into our home that very night and helped her get back on her feet. God never left her, or her son, and they never starved, either. They got back on their feet and are in a better place than before.

So what's the takeaway? In our prayer life, let's pursue a mindset of trust in God's goodness towards us. If you haven't heard it before, here's a verse to help you: Romans 8:28 – "And we know that God works all things together for the good of those who love Him, and are called according to His purpose." Wow. We could have victory over stress and anxiety if we could just grasp the truth in this verse. Overcoming in life isn't just about the big things like cancer and lupus and broken lives; it's in the little places like trust and peace. If you master peace in the small areas, then you can begin to pull that tool from your bag when you face the big tests. Try this. When you're stressed about a situation, go to a solitary place for at least an hour. Just say to God, "I'm stressed, and I need your wisdom and peace." Don't think about the situation, rather speak those verses out loud from Psalm 37:25 and Romans 8:28 in the previous paragraph. Just like the man who said to Jesus, "Lord I believe, but help my unbelief." God will help you and you will walk away with peace and the problem won't seem so big because you got closer to a place of trust.

CHAPTER 12

WHEN YOU'RE BLINDSIDED

Once when I was trying to encourage a friend to believe for a miracle for a pretty bad situation in his life, he became very offended at me and said. "You don't have any idea of the pain that I've suffered and you haven't experienced someone dying in your arms like I have."
His message was that if I knew the depths of real pain, I wouldn't believe so much. He was implying that he had the upper hand on pain and my understanding was naive. I informed him that I held my mother in my arms when she breathed her last breath, her life leaving her body as she died from cancer. I also was only 10 years old when my father passed away from a brain tumor, and a few years ago my wife and I experienced a loss of an unborn child. Even in all this I still believe 100%. In fact, it makes me fight for victory even harder. It encourages me to not be lazy when it comes to prayer.

So what do you do when you are blindsided by loss, when it makes no sense to you? Well maybe this next story will help. In regards to the miscarriage, my wife had a dream a few months earlier. The dream was very simple, but very profound to her. It was simply a very clear profound voice saying to her. "You will name him Samuel." At the time we had no idea that she was pregnant. So she decided to do a pregnancy test, and lo and behold, she was pregnant. It was so exciting for us because we had felt perhaps that we were done with having children after the first two. We had a little late start in life and our second son was born when my wife was 36 years old. Because of the dream we already named the new baby Samuel. We went for the ten week ultrasound with anticipation. When the examination started I noticed something was wrong. The baby just didn't look right, and I could see that he wasn't moving at all. The examiner and I noticed before my wife did. It was a very hard moment. She had miscarried and all we could do was leave the doctor's office through a crowd of waiting people literally with our hands over our faces trying to hide the fact that we were weeping. Although I had experienced the death of both my parents before I was 29 years old, for some reason this pain felt so different, so sudden.

God is the best at taking pain and turning it into joy.

I took my wife home. We just wept. I still had to go to one client meeting that day. On the way home, I asked God a question. I said "God, why would you tell us to name our son Samuel, if he was never going to see a day on earth?" Some people ask,

"How do you know when it's God's voice answering?" My response is that his answer is usually so profound and beyond your understanding, that you never could have thought of that answer. The Lord very clearly answered me. "Steve, who was Samuel in the Bible?" I knew the story of Samuel and that he grew up all his days serving in God's house, because his mother had dedicated him to do so. (1 Samuel 1:21-2:17) So that was my answer to God. "He served you all the days of his life in your house." The Lord responded so clearly to me. "And so your son, Samuel, will also serve all his days in my house here in heaven. He will never feel the pain and difficulty of life on earth."

Joy flooded my heart. I felt such an amazing peace and understanding that I just had to share it. I posted a long post on Facebook about it. I titled it, "The Gift of a Miscarriage". Here is the post from Facebook that very day:

> "The gift of a miscarriage....I must share this deep revelation before time passes and the urgency leaves. My wife and I left the OB today trying to hide the flow of tears today from all the others in the waiting room. The ultrasound at 10 weeks showed that the heartbeat stopped around a week and a half ago. We were so excited before entering the doctor's office to be able to share good news with family and friends, but now we share the opposite......or do we? You see, on my way home from a meeting today I had a revelation

which brings me to the odd caption of "The gift of a miscarriage". Before we even knew Jenny was pregnant she had a vivid dream in which God said "you will name him Samuel." I'll get back to that in a second. Pain of a miscarriage is even a gift because enduring pain makes you more like Jesus because he was "a man familiar with sorrows" and He is "close to the broken hearted" as the Psalms say. I never understood the pain of losing an unborn child until today. I found myself unable to stop the flow of tears, Jenny no less. So what about Samuel? I realized today why his name is Samuel. Who was Samuel in the Bible? His mother dedicated him to serve the Lord "all his days" in God's temple. Now our Samuel will never live a day on Earth, but he is with God serving Him forever in His heavenly temple. He is a son with a purpose dedicated to God. And finally knowing all this, I can also say to those who don't value the life of unborn children: Is my little Samuel not significant because he hasn't exited the womb? Hardly. He is a gift. And his loss is a gift. Our gift to God if we choose to be thankful. And we are. It is so much better to live life with a thankful heart than one of bitterness and questioning.

I really don't believe it's ever God's original plan to lose a child, but I do know that God is the best at taking pain and turning it into joy. We now have four children in our house and two in heaven (my 2nd son had a twin that didn't make it, either). What a joy life is, and I get to meet two more of my children in heaven someday, because we have put our faith in what Jesus has done for us on the cross. God is good. I wouldn't trade my pain for a minute, for there is so much joy that I have received on the other side of it. I know some of you have had severe pain, or are experiencing it right now. When you're blindsided, know that your joy will be complete when you have Jesus. It's always good to get to know Him while you're here on Earth. It helps your understanding of this life because you end up with His heart in yours.

CHAPTER 13

BATTLES WON

Earlier I mentioned that when things got to their worst point in Jacob's illness, I became determined to never give up praying, just like the persistent widow. I was like a weary fighter knocked down in the corner with my opponent raising his hands prematurely in assumed victory. But with a surge of defiance and determination to believe we could win this battle, I got up and prayed like never before.

After only a few days of praying like this, I woke up in the morning and looked at my son's face while he was still sleeping. The lesions had diminished 80% overnight. My son's face and entire body began to clear so quickly. I was actually seeing the results of the battle, the final battle for my son's healing. I had done like David had done. I had encouraged myself in the Lord and I went to the enemy's camp and took back what he had stolen from me. It took a while, a lot of tears, not eating, and battling in prayer, but the victory was near... and I could see it.

There's one thing I hadn't explained yet. We had to wait several months from the time of making the appointment with the rheumatologist, before we were actually able to see her. I had prayed from the beginning that Jacob would be healed already by the time we went to the appointment. The reason I prayed this was so that we could get medical verification of his healing. So this story could be a verified healing and not simply my word about it. By the time I saw the radical change in my son's appearance overnight, the doctor's appointment was only 2 days away!

We went to the doctor's appointment that Thursday. When we got there, the doctor really couldn't see much more visible evidence of his lesions, because they had faded almost completely. But she explained that from the evidence in his previous blood tests, his level of antinuclear antibodies were very high. She recommended that we start him on Plaquenil, which is a medication for treating lupus symptoms, with potential side effects. I asked her if it was a lifelong prescription. She replied that it was a lifelong treatment. But I knew in my heart that he wouldn't need it. We already had the victory. So before the Plaquenil could be given, another set of complete blood tests were needed to check DNA and other more specific disorders. That day they took 13 vials of blood from my little boy's arm. I just knew that the test results would show that he was fine, but there was still a waiting period.

Two weeks passed, and we heard no news from the doctor. After such an agonizing wait, I just told my wife to contact them and ask for the results. I remember the moment and place I received the call from my wife crying. "Honey! He's normal!" She said while crying. "All the tests came back normal! Jacob is healed!" I have heard it said that the strongest emotion in all of humanity isn't love or joy or pain. Rather the strongest emotion is the feeling of relief. I can't tell you the relief I felt knowing that my son was healed.

We actually hold in our hands the medical records which initially show evidence of an autoimmune disease, and the results of the final blood tests which show every level normal. We've never had an issue since, and it's been almost two years since that happened. Our lives are completely normal. No medication, no lesions, no rashes and no more doctor's visits. Victory won, battle over! Thank you Jesus for your power!

I hope that before you even get to this point in the book, you've already become determined to start praying like never before. We've been taught to model Jesus' life by the way we serve, love and sacrifice for others. Let's also remember that Jesus often went to solitary places to pray and be with his father, God. Start today to model Jesus' life of prayer. There's a rich life awaiting you there at the top of the mountain in God's presence, hearing from him, being encouraged by His Word and sitting next to Him in heavenly places. You are an heir or heiress to a life of total victory.

CHAPTER 14

YOU'RE LONGING FOR SOMETHING

The other day, I was telling many of these stories of answered prayer, and hearing God's voice to a friend at her workplace. She said to me, "I just wish I could have what you have." My response to her was, "You can have as much of Jesus as you want." All of these changes in my life, since the prayer challenge I did six years ago, are based on a deepening relationship between my Father in heaven and myself. God originally intended our relationship with him to be pure and unhindered, just like Adam and Eve in the book of Genesis. But as the rest of the scriptures show, all the way up to Jesus' coming, things had gotten messier. Relationships were broken and things that God never wanted to be part of our lives, such as murder, hate and greed, entered into the world. This is why God had to send Jesus to take all the messiness and evil in the world and place it on himself and die on the cross. It was an incredible love for us and a desire to bring reconciliation to our relationship that he did this. And what's our part? There's no complicated formula or specific prayer, as some would have you believe, that allows us to be restored to a relationship with the One who made us. The most simple example is when Jesus was dying on the cross, the criminal being crucified next to him said,

> "Jesus, remember me when you come into your kingdom." [43] And he [Jesus] said to him, "Truly, I say to you, today you will be with me in paradise."

This simple phrase from the criminal signified that he believed and recognized who Jesus was. This small act of faith, in essence, was his salvation moment. Romans 10:9-10 is our road map to restoration with God, as it reads:

> [9] because, if you confess with your mouth that Jesus is Lord and believe in your heart that God raised him from the dead, you will be saved. [10] For with the heart one believes and is justified, and with the mouth one confesses and is saved."

So if you're saying to yourself, like my friend said to me, "I just wish I had what you have," my answer is, "You can." God doesn't need any special formula to give you the love you need and the power to overcome. Just believe in Him and what Jesus did for you. I know that God is able to speak for Himself to someone who really wants to know Him. Do you want to know how I know this? Let me tell you one final story...

I was living in China studying the language and I had a

friend who lived there (in the city of Xi'An). The Chinese national stance on God is, well, there isn't one. They're officially atheists. However, I wanted to introduce my friend to God, because I know God loves him, and just like the rest of us, he wants his children back. Because of language barriers I knew that I couldn't effectively communicate who God was with him, so I just asked him if he believed that there was a God. He replied, "I don't know, but I really want to know if God is real." This was the perfect opportunity. I was not going to preach to him, or tell him anything. All I did was give him one simple instruction. I said to him, "If you want to know if God is real, just ask him. Tonight while you're riding your bike home, ask God if He is real and ask Him to show you that He is. If He's real, He will tell you."   I knew God would reveal himself to my friend because his nature is to love His children.

I didn't hear from my friend for more than 2 weeks. I was wondering what happened that night. Did he ask God? Did he hear anything? Well – I received a phone call from him two weeks later. He was so excited on the phone he could hardly contain himself. He said to me, "Stephen, you remember that night when I left your apartment? On the way home I asked God if he was real. I went to bed that night, and in my sleep I was suddenly lifted up into the sky with such a rush. I felt this warmth and sense of love, then suddenly I was back in my bed. I asked, God, 'If that was you, do it again.' Then just as suddenly as before, I was rushed up into the sky and there was that warmth and love again. This time I felt a hand brush across my forehead like a parent would to a child. I never felt such love in all my life." At that moment my friend knew beyond a shadow of a doubt that God was real and loved him. I was able to introduce him to his Heavenly Father and reconnect him with his Creator without even preaching a word. I just opened the opportunity for introduction.

Right now, as you read this, I'm opening the opportunity for you to be introduced to your Father in heaven. He is showing you the pathway to restoration, which is simply believing that Jesus already took your wrongs and your pain and died for you. Just ask God to show you that He is real, and if you're open to knowing Him, I know He will do just that. When you find Him, or He finds you, however you want to look at it, you can begin to pursue Him in prayer just like I did, and begin to walk on this journey of total victory. May God bless you richly.

ACKNOWLEDGEMENTS

Many miracles would have never taken place on this planet had it not been for Jamie Gardner, my pastor for 9 years at Praise Assembly. Pastor Jamie – you challenged me to start the prayer challenge that changed my life. Through it, so many victories have been won. People have been healed from migraines, cancer, lupus, juvenile rheumatoid arthritis, and many other physical problems. Families have been restored and people have come to Christ, all because you opened my eyes to the wonder of pursuing God with everything I have.

To the Kuelkers who walked with us through so many situations and prayed with us, you helped us make it through some of the most difficult moments, and for that, your family has such a precious place in our hearts.

Ed Moonen, thank you for praying for us and continuing to be a rock while we transitioned to California. You've always been such an amazing encouragement. The words you spoke over me during the last few years gave me the courage to write down in this book what God has done in our lives.

Lifelong friends are hard to find, nearly impossible, actually. The Heaths are more precious than a treasure chest full of gold. There's millions of pounds of gold on the planet, but there's only one Slade and one Tiffany (And we couldn't forget their amazing kids, too).

The Hamiltons. Chris, young Jedi, always use your powers for good and not evil. You bunch of weirdos who live in a train, you're the only family that came all the way to California just to visit us. (Twice!) We love you. Your friendship has carried us a long way.

Lisa Marchetta, when I first read the book after you added your touch and finesse for the English language, I cried tears of joy. You truly are a great friend. Thank you for the many, many hours spent making this book what it is.

ABOUT THE AUTHOR

This picture of the Wollwerth family was taken at the spot where Stephen went everyday to pray for his son's healing. It's also the place where God revealed some of the secrets of finding encouragement through God's word. Stephen and his wife Jenny live in Folsom California with their 3 sons and a beautiful little daughter. Stephen is the owner of a film and video production company called 3GatesFilms, which does production work for a variety of commercial clients as well as non-profits. He has been an editor and director of photography for a national PBS television show, as well as the media director for several churches. The greatest passion for Stephen is to be able to make a difference in showing God's power and love through video production and writing.

If you want to email Stephen with questions or comments, email: wollwerth@gmail.com